THE SCENT OF WATER

poems by
Patricia Barone

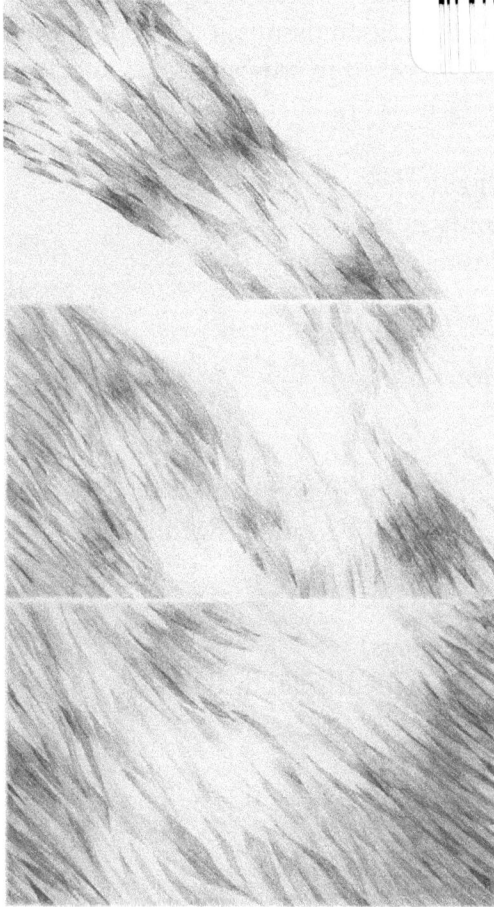

BLUE LIGHT PRESS ◆ 1ST WORLD PUBLISHING

1st WORLD
PUBLISHING

SAN FRANCISCO ◆ FAIRFIELD ◆ DELHI

THE SCENT OF WATER

Copyright ©2013 by Patricia Barone

BLUE LIGHT PRESS
www.bluelightpress.com
Email: bluelightpress@aol.com

BOOK DESIGN:
Melanie Gendron

COVER ART:
(horizontal inset: a triptych of drawings)
"River Reed Triptych" by Elizabeth Bachhuber

INTERIOR ART:
(the individual drawings)
"River Reed Triptych" by Elizabeth Bachhuber

PHOTOGRAPHS:
of the Author and the Drawings (Cover and Interior)
Matthew Giovinetti

FIRST EDITION

LCCCN: 2013911408

ISBN: 978-1-4218-8670-1

PUBLICATION ACKNOWLEDGMENTS

Thank you to the editors who published these poems, some with different titles in earlier versions, in the following publications:

American Poetry Journal, No. 9: "January Candelabra"
Earth's Daughters: "We Lived, We Made Preserves"
Future Cycle: "The Ferris Wheel"
Germination (Canada): "Rounding the Arc," "Writing a Poem With Claire, Who is Almost Four"; the latter poem was reprinted in *Zeit Raum*, a catalog of art by Christoph Rihs (Germany), and *Elementary Language Arts Instruction, Prentice Hall*
Great River Review: "Retrieval," "Eminent Domain," "How We Come to Settle on the River"
Loonfeather: "The Balance"
Mankato Poetry Review: "Domesticity"
Momentum: "An Invitation to Diffusion"
North County Anvil: "Our Mooring"
Pleiades: "Flying Through the Ring of the Seasons"
Poets On: Arriving "The Chain Letter Promises"
An Sionnach: "Seeing Through This World"
Seattle Review: "Trail Song for the Third Millennium"
Streamlines: "Fundamental Music"
Tendril: "Standing Ground," "Survival," "The River Refuses to Waive Its Lien"
The Prose Poem Project: "A Guest in Your own Shell"
And the Humming: poems about grandparents, Trotter's Café series, "Muddle Along"
Visions International: "Palimpsest"
War and Peace, from *Little Monster Press:* "Pandora's Boxes of Perverted Words"
Yarrow: "When the Hibernation Moon begins to Rise," "The Oracle"

THANK YOU TO ALL THE PEOPLE WHO HELPED MAKE THIS BOOK POSSIBLE:

Known for work inspired by environmental issues, artist Elizabeth Bachhuber, Professor of Sculpture and Installation at the Faculty of Art and Design, Bauhaus-University, Weimar, Germany, has exhibited throughout Europe and the United States. The cover and interior images are from her drawings, *River Reed Triptych*, pencil on paper;

Photographer Matthew Giovinetti, who is Director of Photography, The Food Network, and Director of the program, *Diners, Drive-ins, and Dives*;

Onionskin writing group members (1978–2013) commented on many of these poems in early drafts: Sharon Chmielarz, Kate Dayton, Diane Jarvi, Norita Dittberner-Jax, Dorian Kottler, Laura Littleford, Margaret Hasse, Tom Heie, Sue Ann Martinson, Carol Masters, Martha Meek, Paula Moyer, Nancy Raeburn, Barbara Sperber, Cary Waterman; and Mary Kay Rummel, for her many close readings of the manuscript.

Diane Frank, whose workshop inspired many of these poems; and the participating writers who shared their work and insights.

Faith Sullivan, mentor-friend extraordinaire, and her Wednesday afternoon class members, for their constant help and support: Sandy Bloom, Connie Kunin, Nancy Massman, Mary McLeod, Barb Strandel, and Eileen Welsh. In fond memory of Eleanor Waldrup.

Kay Cavanaugh Barnes, friend, writer, and sister-traveler on significant life journeys; Mary Beth Craft, friend and writer, whose encouragement and example are an inspiration; Sue Johnson and Linda Wing, who remind me that writing and life are artful play;

Michael Dennis Browne, John Minczeski, and Jim Moore, early mentor-teachers. Jean Ervin and Chet Corey of *Great River Review*, who nominated "Retrieval" for a Pushcart Prize;

Britt Fleming and members of Northography.com, who will recognize the visual inspiration for four of these poems. "Keen for New Orleans" and "Blake's Beautiful Failure," were posted in early drafts on the Northography web site.

Forever and always to the inspiration of my life and this book: I am grateful for the love and support of my husband, Stan; my children, Matthew and Claire; and my brothers and sisters, with whom I share many formative experiences and values;
Tim, Steve, Dan, Liz, Mary, and Tom
in memory of our parents
and brother Eddie.

For Stan, Matt, and Claire

TABLE OF CONTENTS

Tenancy

End Notes

TAP ROOT

Your Test

The little things catch first
and rip like tiny stitches in a wound.

Spitting embers sting your legs—
your feet are scorched by flames.

You dither, unable
to choose that brooch, will, shoe—
they're all the same.

You neglected to practice for your life,
never gripping the extinguisher's red ring—
now yank the pin! You fail to aim.

Your smoke alarm wails as you run in place
suffering from mad preoccupation—
Photos! Thumb drive! Will!

You pull your daughter from her bed.
Shoeless, your son and husband
drag the dog through sleet.

Though everyone you love is a survivor,
you have a terrible need,
so you look back.

Once in a Limestone Cave

I tripped on the rock of prophecy.
Refusing to put it down
until it answered me,
I asked, *Where will I live?*

Squeezed like a sponge,
it gushed ancient seas
but would not speak.

Then from the sclerotic skeleton
I held between my hands,
creatures emerged:
an armadillo, a chalk-white rat,
a mollusk and a grieving bonobo.
I asked them, *please, where shall I live?*

Mute, the armadillo crept in armor all day long
across the Tung Plantation road to guard
wild horses drinking the moon
in the springtide pool. *You'll live*
where you arrive most slowly.

The rodent lifted his snoot
from the burrows of his dolomite maze.
You'll live where you learn.

The elephant mussel quivered,
a mirage disappearing into rugae,
the vagina. *You'll live in many folds.*

Yes, I said, *but where?*
The bonobo's tears reflected
the back of her brain, festooned
with creatures of the jungle. *You'll live
where you are crowded with your life.*

Domesticity

for my husband

Asparagus, like a cat,
is found by chance.
The spears we peeled
were sweet and unforeseen—
less innocent than corn,
a darker aftertaste, like ale.

Wild cannot be owned
and we grew weary
eating field stalks gone to seed,
thick of skin in ditches.

We grew albino ones,
more tender than the green,
deep in leaf-mold trenches,
filled with kitchen compost,
a harem kept in purdah.

When we glanced away,
their plump fingers thinned
and thrust the soil aside.
Ivory crowns gone mauve,
engorged on sun, turned lime
and measured us in our brief summer.

We Lived and Made Preserves

Leaving the camaraderie of the all-night laundry,
we trailed our roots between New Orleans and St. Paul
and settled in a country farmhouse. Its slanted floors
sent our borrowed washer spinning to the wall.
Our stairs were so narrow we heaved
the mattress in the window. Midges sifted
our love sounds through the screen.

Once friends on our porch swing kissed goodbye,
a sad-moist sound. We pretended not to listen.
When heavy air snapped with summer hail,
and wind snatched shutters, we laughed—
Our next door neighbor upended,
tying burlap on a rose bush.
He yelled at his wife— "*You* can nest
on your friggin' grandiflora!"

They ran, but we didn't descend our cellar stairs,
built for onions, pickles, sauer kraut and tornadoes.
We huddled under eaves, drinking brandy,
as gusts lifted petunias, oak leaves,
bamboo rakes and crows.

The rain sluiced gutters,
but we didn't know disaster.
Rutabagas floated from the garden to the steps,
and bobbed like buoys beneath our feet

Fundamental Music

On the same sunburned lawn, I hope for a message.
The postman's off-key droning whistle drifts our block.
Our mailbox gapes, less like eating than yawning.

At the symphony I wait, expecting the final repetition
in another key. Brass or, in the *1812*, a cannon.

Pathetique concludes so quietly. Like a cricket hiding
in our November cellar, whose diapause aria fades
to rusty chirps then silence near our furnace.

Our toddler in the rocker on the porch, its drowsy creaking.
He smacks his sneakers on the siding, slows and sleeps.

Walking, a dance of shifting feet. One foot meets the earth,
as the other lifts and swings through air, off-balance—
the syncopated rhythm of a heartbeat.

Our Mooring

for Stan

Once we strapped on snow shoes, the island was accessible on ice.
Now, as we swim through sleep, the wind begins to float our house.
Remember turning the canoe, paddles flat against the fluent band
of current? Mooring our boat above the pebbled sand, we climbed
as far as the preserve, our trespass guided by the moon.

When brambles filled the dells on level ground, we perched
our tent upon a gentle slope and slept until lightning, shearing air,
printed birch on our cloth walls, and we woke—torrents breached
the hill, carving gullies beneath our canvas boat. Listen to the river—
turtles crevice into rocks, and black birds thread the rain.

Muddle Along

Your mind, in dailiness,
is like the kitchen drawer—
gummy pencils, pumpkin seeds,
disorder too innocuous to change.

The garden does not need you.
Creeping to your window, corn
is breathing ancient carbon.
You lie in the night and just listen.

When you vacation, Crowder peas
reach across to strangle weeds.
When you return, a jungle makes
weeding incidental to the harvest.

Think of the mistakes you've made,
unsure for a moment what they are.

Rounding the Arc

Purple-black eggplants
flow to the soil all summer.
Seeds grow heavy and fall
the way eggs grow—oval, slow.

Limestone water drips
in the rain barrel, corn crib,
as Salmon Cockerels usher
Bantam Buff Orpington hens.

Dusty Orange Cornish follow
Silver Pencil roosters, and the flock
strews feathers quill side down
in an evening garden.

Yolks revolve in albumin.
Small suns thicken the air
as each beam cools
to bone and rises plume.

Guinea cocks' red combs,
their match-tip eyes,
spark phosphorescence
on the steel-blue sky.
Guinea hens scratch and glow.

The Balance

In Breughel's painting, wheat
wide-swathed, a hot-amber tunnel curves,
and the workers drowse.
It's autumn, the spell
between a desolation of roses
and a melon's perfect revolution.
Days warm in a shallow pool,
and nights defer the frost.

A boy jumps from straw in the mow
to the loaves of hay below.
From the vast loft, he leaps
and is caught by light.

Bruised by the sun, a plum bursts.
Water forced up turgid stems
splits cabbages. It's almost time
for picking, but wait—

Pollen-dusted children
slumber in the shade.
It's noon, and the day ripens.

When the Hibernation Moon Begins to Rise,

the hummingbird's nightly torpor
hoards her energy for day.
She cantilevers flowers,
whirrs her wings in place.

If winter came to me each night
I wouldn't need this house, my cave,
its birch and maple fires to burn the winter low.
I hate the tyranny of windows.

A herd of foraging white-tail bucks—
their bright hindquarters
our planet's shooting stars—
take turns bounding over
nothing at all.

Without their silver sheathes,
willow buds would freeze.
Scilla bulbs curve
on a lathe of snow.

The rabbit's tracks circle
broken wind breaks, then she burrows
deep to earth and lines her nest with fur
she pulls from haunch and flank.

Her long doze ended, she gives birth
to tiny conies, blind and hairless,
beneath the long-eared
hare moon.

The Ineffable Thing

remembering my children's first words

The shape of your mouth, the way
your lips close and hum
then open for a burst
of exhaled breath—your first round *mahm*.

Summoning honey, your tongue
withdraws to your soft palate; your tone
vibrates through your nose
when you beg for milk.

How your tongue curls up
around *bird*!
Bees, a plosive puff,
buzz vibrations in your throat.

A fish zips out as you echo me—*fish*!
Then it is gone and you suspect
a sleight of my big hands.

Another goldfish swims beneath your nose,
and you say *thing*!—your tongue between your teeth—
thing! The shell-like word we humans use

to hold what our tongues cannot catch—
a shape alters light,
fleeting shadows whisk
around the corners of our minds.

Maybe a magician's trick,
a sort of thimblerig:
As if beneath three cups,
rocks, hats, or waving kelp,
you don't find the hidden thimble—

only azure feathers, gold-leaf flecks
of fin in rushing water.

Writing a Poem With Claire, Who is Nearly Four

The winter bears come out
when ice stops the river.

And trees on the island look
like broken teeth on a comb?

No! It's hair sticking up
from a giant papa bear.
His forehead's cold,
and his dreams got frozen.

His little bears won't take their naps.
They crawl through a hole in the snow
and make angel wings on his stomach.

What does the giant hear?
Do you think white sounds
like a whisk broom,
or the brush on a snare drum?

A bear drum's a big log.
When mother bear sweeps. . .

Snow off the island's back?
Or do the bears roll up the snow?

They do it with their fur,
but first she hits the log
and gets the giant up.

Mom, write this:
in spring when bears wake up,
I'll color them red and yellow,
and they'll be caterpillars.

Flying Through the Ring of the Seasons

Stay with me. . . if you can do all kinds of housework well, I shall be very pleased. But you must be very particular how you make my bed; it must be thoroughly shaken, so that the feathers fly, then it snows. . . . I am Mother Hulda.
—Sixty Fairy Tales of the Brothers Grimm

Winging down the continent,
we shatter cirrus strata.
Below, the bound Mississippi
frees our lives—ice explodes,
and snow-packed gravel grinds the banks.
Fish gush up from the ice crack,
once sealed over like a scar.
From the outlet to the north shore,
the pick axe slices and glaciers calve.
The crystal jet spumes, each puff imploding,
sound no barrier above—jet engines rupture
each cracking ring of hoar frost.

A wrecking ball, a battering ram! *At 7 a.m., Mother Hulda's*
picture window on the river shatters—a runaway wedge
of ice like a crowbar that lifts and shifts, abrading the levee.

Melt torques her dwelling south. Was she
invaded by winter or spring?
Above, a boom like an echo of the thaw.

Mother Hulda covers her ears, looks up, and shakes her head.
Mortals who leave before she's shaken the down in her pillows—
those slackers gripe her soul. She leans on her shovel
and glares at her over-stocked living room.

Underneath us, white gives way
to saffron and green,
as if the fuselage released
the seasons, cylinders of a telescope.

We're hanging, the plane a balloon;
then the pilot dives—
the drop in pressure
implodes our inner ears,
each cochlear channel ringing
the whorl of every chambered Nautilus,
as we descend too fast and land in summer.

Mother Hulda sweeps her stairs and steppes,
and melts the hardened permafrost.

All we left we carried with us—our heads
preserve the winter. Like refugees, we're slow
to shed our wraps and nurse our colds with heat.
Then we reach the ocean's breezes, where surf
catches sandpipers wading on double-jointed legs.

Holding whelk shells to our ears, we hear
blood in cadence with the undersides of waves.
Reflecting gray-blue sky, they curl

dandelion wine and celadon
green—they break in whispers,
respiration of the tides.

We who flew beneath her lofty gate,
afraid of Mother Hulda's tar, are altered.

The tiny cilia, blown down in flight,
stir the semi-circular canals,
secret pools of the ear. We hear
the roar, the coins of light on water.
We reel beneath the sun.

Our leaning bodies, wounded gyroscopes,
tilt—we dance our little dance off balance
then lie down on shingles, swept clear
by breakers, leaving cowrie,
coral, jellyfish and conch.

When Life Is a Cupboard of Moments

for Ueli and Regula; Graubünden, Switzerland

My world is a patchwork cabin
full of querulous voices.
I wake before the needy day.

After scraping my porridge bowl,
I walk in *Nebel*, a mist so thick
it is the floor of time.

Fog sleeves itself, tears on a peak.
I slide between rents—below me,
snails lay gleaming tracks.
Rain is their condition.

Descending the saddle ridge,
I follow the conchiolin arks of escargot
far from the conches of the ocean.

Eyes on stalks, they nudge the air,
testing wind resistance.

Wrinkling feet, they glide on slime
over granite, slate, obsidian.

Knowing I'd never out-pace the snails,
I don't falter when *Nebel* erases
past, future, even my steep path.

Crawling when I can't see,
I feel ancient grains of volcanic glass
fuse beneath my calloused hands:

Time's mirror, the crossing place we share
with snails, which flow without moving,
in pace with the movement of mountains.

Eminent Domain

1.

In our first garden, I thought I made
the friable top layer, though it was a farmer's
loam and labor—a good soil.

New owners laid sod on sweet marjoram,
pebble mulch on mint. My Easter lilies lie
beneath their asphalt.

Let bush balsam's fuzzy seeds all hatch
and teem like poppies in their turf—
a permanence for transient roots.

2.

On our second mini-parcel,
I harrow and weed the windrow
between our house and the one next door.
The parachutes from cotton trees and dandelions
float down to root in welcome mats.
Nature is a maniac for sperm.

Like butterflies, peach columbines
hover plum violas. Loganberries leave
abandoned lots for ours. Gloriosa daisies throng,
gamboge and maroon. Unlike a great-cat tamer,
I don't flick a whip, but wield my shears
on pods that carry seeds. Tiger lilies snarl
in red and black, and leopard lilies leap
through August's final hoop.

3.

As the children grow they shinny higher
in our gnarly oak, their goal for summer—
an abandoned eagle's nest, a tawny feather.

Each spring I feed and hoe the old rugosa rose,
pink clusters small as Brussels sprouts,
one sturdy cane for the coming year.

If we're still here. The county plans to pour
concrete piles for a cable bridge. To sink the caisson
off our bank, they'd scrape our acre of elms and home,
scouring topsoil, seeding the aster patch with window glass.

4.

Only the Mississippi's easement—
through a few dozen families, lilac bushes—
is honored by us. It doesn't seize without deposit.
The river surges, tops the bank, and sands our floors.
Leaving arms from neighbors' chairs, it transfers
things that float through transoms.

Our old neighbor won't budge:
"This is my place." It is—
He still has hand-tied trout flies,
salmon mayflies, caddis flies of cat fur,
and royal fan-wings underneath
a ton of sludge in spring.

Periwinkle slip in mud,
air and fire stump, water.
That's what he means by home.

How We Come to Settle on the River

for my husband

I sleepwalk up the stairs before you.
When sun is just a gray mist in our room,
you rise for me without alarm.
Devouring Swiss fondue,
we talk of foreign travel.

As a charm, I pick some coral mushrooms.
Their gills are pleated by each breeze,
yet fold back in, sautéed
in chives and olive oil.

One four a.m., a dream of thwarted passage
wakes me—an angel, feathers made of tin,
tinseled heels, each flap of wing
coded on a microchip.

"Too much traffic here," you say. "I can't sleep
when you're thinking." I'm not surprised you hear
pacing phantoms in loose armor.
I tune you to my frequency.

Your nightmare: you keep reaching up to pluck
dull butter knives from air before they hit us.
The poltergeist suggests we journey on?

No, my love—this house subsides with us,
wrinkles and a plaster crack or two.
We're sinking through the river silt to bedrock.

Now lodged in a striation of the sandstone cliff,
our vantage point half chosen, we remain
a tuning fork for the seasons.

After You Lose Your Map

Grip the willow branch
twitching over fault lines,

then follow each dip of twig
until it bends so far

it sends down roots
to retrieve the scent of water.

Cyclone

How the Race Becomes a Dance

On the last October Sunday at the track,
we wrap ourselves in blankets, clutch
thermoses and watch the blue flames lick
from Sterno cooking stoves. We practice luck.
Our blasphemy is Chance, another name
for God, who just might favor

Buns Galore Lady-of-the-Sky   Madame Bovary
Crafty Storm   King Drone   Reign Road.

As touts smoke Tiparillos, they pretend
to study racing forms, as if their god
helps those who do their homework.
Expert divination is feeling
taut rope beneath bare toes,
the dancer swaying his pole
between leap and fall.

This thread is wide
through the narrow gate
that *Wicked Wit* is streaking past.
Baby-It's-Hot-Outside regains the inside curve.
As *Damelo* and *Meadow Flyer* bring us to our feet,
Cash Legacy moves up, but I put my bucks—all ten—
on a nag who bolts from the starting bell
to lag a distant tenth. I picked him
for his name—*Irritation.*

Standing Ground

Feathers flung over jagged corn,
wild geese beat their wings
against a cobalt sky.

Each year we're drawn
to the marsh
as far as we dare.

The skein of geese descends
faster, lower than before.

This year a feather,
hollow quill tipped with blood,
cut my cheek like paper.

Listening to the Oracle

Crickets thrum warmth
out of time, their lento drone
between my shoulder blades.
Cold icing wings, they hover—
a knife-shaped cloud.

Now my body turns to listen
with the pores of my skin
to the moment silence rises, reaches my eyes—
the northern lights, where spirits dance

and crickets play each other's wings,
drawing their forewing bows
on hindwing strings to swell
the massive cricket body's
climbing treble,
contrapuntal hum.

Grace

The fires we built that winter
were feeble and scanned
the newspapers in one scorch,
leaving each sheet whole but charred.
Black words dropped into the cinders.

Pine kept its cold green heart,
bark gnawed by futile matches.
Both miserly and poor,
we wore our overcoats indoors.
You rolled string. I grudged
the mice each crumb.

Late March we laid a pyre,
hard new oak on balsam.
The log drizzled sap, cracked sparks,
and blazed as smoke possessed our room—
we'd forgotten to open the damper.

After dousing our fiasco with weak tea,
we turned our backs on the soggy grate
and waited for the hearth to dry.

We could have scraped the bricks
or gathered sticks, but we were weary,
being in a constant shiver, feeling mean.

Yellow flickering stirred the embers,
and we bent to warm our hands
on one kindling coal.

The Book Reads You

You enter a novel, complicit
with the characters, your fictional family.

You're enchanted with the way
he reads poetry to please her.

She reminds their child,
"your daddy's tired."

The parents take turns nursing him
nights he cries with an earache.

Bereft, you aren't prepared
for their divorce—how absurd
retracing the small clues you missed:

her shrunken chapter in the trash,
the subscription he forgets to cancel.

Credit overdrawn and blind on whiskey,
he's totaled on the toll road home.

"Why grieve for fictional people?"
your husband asks, and you say,
"It's wrong for their child to die,
after all the nights they tucked him in."

Overcautious, the parents tried
to give their child freedom, then didn't
warn him of murderous strangers.
They couldn't evade the writers plan.

Your pain too personal to be art,
you think you could avert
the partings of your life
were you a better reader.

The Chain Letter Promises

money in geometric progression,
prayers, dirty post cards,
a lewd or meretricious proposal,
a cure for emphysema.

You expect these things
to drop through the slot in your life.

Week by week uncounted correspondents
let go or tumble off, and it veers.

Your private circle of words
multiplies into years,
bleached of menace—
a snake with its tail in its mouth.

Seeing Through This World

Samhain in America

Streetlight to streetlight,
through oil-slicked puddles,
no one removes a mask.

Inside, I slice chocolates,
and no one asks questions.
No glass in the caramel.
No razor in the cake.

Claire in her pink tutu pirouettes
to Offenbach's Bluebeard.
As she unwinds her spin,
my old Polaroid steals her whirl.

A flash and she emerges from the cloud—
green morphing peach, her hands
cupped above her head, her gauzy dress
blanched white, each black eyelash etched
then thinned, skin pallid, exposed.

As the trumpets fade,
the ghosts and clowns stop capering.

I pluck their sticky image out—
Children rising from the photo
forget to smile.

Looking back an era later,
by minutes or a century, we see

how Claire's arm lifts
and curves at the elbow, arabesque,
as she holds the poisoned apple of the world.

Pandora's Boxes of Perverted Words

CLOUD

The purple ogre says, *Hi!*
in my daughter's drawing.
Where did Claire learn monsters
are tame, except from me?

Mine is gray. Peering up at him,
I see: *Everything's too big,*
written on mushroom clouds,
erased words—*refined interrogation,*
collateral damage, winnable nuclear war.

MATRIX

Official words are beige.
Their inoffensive tones
don't warn but form
cooling vessels for the core
of red words, ~~meltdown~~,
unscheduled event,
in the *containment area.*
Matrix used to mean womb.

Grille

Griddle melts the tar beneath
bare feet running from monsters.
Claire's beast howls—"His teeth hurt."
My monster screams for nerve gas,
voice pitched beyond the human ear.
He can't taste or see our blood,
unless there is a lot of it, requiring
special rendition, ~~torture~~ in *black sites.*

Net

My tongue is numb.
Like stroke patients, we
are left with just our syntax,
a sieve dropping concrete nouns.
Who is drawing finer nets for living words—
my *child,* your *pulse,* our *mother?*

Production Notes for a War Movie

BACK STORY—USE OLD FOOTAGE:

For our remake of a 1940s classic,
say goodbye as they did—too soon.
When anyone inhales a cigarette,
the sky, like paper, smolders from the center
and Mars rips through the haze.

Down our streets and steps, men fail—
dropping keys, short of breath.
Handshakes, hugs, farewells
all stall as they uncoil,
scorching their film,
the little time we haven't.

CLIMAX—USE OLD FOOTAGE AND NEW:

Plucky newsmen capture gore
despite flaming cameras,
tearing sprockets.
When celluloid melts,
keep mothers rushing through
black charred doorways
for their children.

For IMAX, shoot black holes
engulfing our globe, its wireless skies
and plunging drones. Sound tracks speed away
in silent space—human voices die.

Then cell by cell, we'll fade: no streaming images
of life—will we have light?

CONCLUSION—ALL NEW:

After fire-storm winds,
the wheat is ash upon the verge.
As once stooped workers beat the grain
releasing chaff from seed,

will our armored tanks return
to flail the ground with iron chains,
exploding the fields, saving a few
of the lives we mined?

Keen for New Orleans

eight years after the Katrina flood

What is the common hinge
the black winds swing upon?

They ran beneath the falling sky,
as hurricane inhaled the ocean.
No light pierced the undersides
of whirling clouds;
no god broke through
the frangible panes of windows—
only sand and water.

Lightning seared the shores
along the Gulf of Mexico.
Our leader, intent on war,
brewed firestorms in Iraq.

Back home, his helicopter high
above the torrent, he did not
descend to visit the flooded land,
or lower his eyes to the bodies,
bloated Ninth-Ward faces
floating lower Canal
beneath the stinking sun,
lives receding in the waters' rise.

No one looked for the common hinge
the black winds swing upon.

Missing the Signs

Under the soughing wind,
we heard the cry that grass blades make
between the lips—a hoarse whistle.

A woodpecker's ratchet-drill
cut off. Chainsaws rasped and whined
under the falling canopy.
The last tree crashed.

Remember swallows whisking past—
light splintered in trifocal prisms
on our morning papers.

We turned the pages,
pressed their shadows—
feathers, leaves.

A Guest in Your Own Shell

Once you were the love root, white-forked May apple,
skinned mandrake.

Now your shower stall is an aqueduct sinking in the fens,
and water flows rusty.

When you rise, your second story porch stretches
halfway around the sky.

In former days you took a turn beneath the eaves,
growing taller with each step.

Only this roofless room was big enough
to ease you, but now

fissures in beams sponge rain, creating
punky nests for ants.

Morning glories, poking their quick tendrils
between planks,

turn back to weave the fence, their cerulean
discs too heavy.

You used to sit upon your deck to commune
with the river.

Now your mouth full of nails, you prepare your house
for your absence.

Now the Eggplant Plummets in Slow Motion

1.

The planet tips.
Your plot, a spare quarter acre,
edges away from the sun.

It will freeze tonight if air at sunset
has the tang of tarragon,

if pike dart the shallows of northern lakes,
if hard stars threaten.

The moon's in sudden focus—
your depth of field shows ice
to infinity or Orion's belt.

2.

Tending basil and twelve tomatoes
straining to be fed,

you wish for a walled herbarium
beyond the frontier frost.

To reach safe center,
you water fragile vines and make
crystal chandeliers of unripe honeydew.

3.

In crack the whip, our human team
spins around the pivot.

The final skater grips a hand,
and the leader snaps the chain
to launch him into space.

If he's tardy, the window to Mars
locks for a trillion light years,
a better alignment.

4.

A pilot, veteran of eighty hurricanes,
speaks of the eye-wall: *You ride out
the down drafts and up drafts,
gravity twice over.*

5.

You think there is a universe
between the fall and winter:
one moment where you try
to save your life.

Palimpsest

In second sight I scatter ashes
to fertilize the winter radish.
I strain to see the earth or feel it
but only meet the silky grit of soot.
The ground I tried to till was theirs.
Fire consumed their future.

Beneath the hawthorn tree's pink flowers,
I hold my small son's hand and gaze at the lake,
past their house imprinted on the air.

When Matt was an infant, his fists, like buds, curled tight.
I couldn't lift one of his fingers without releasing them all.

Sun in layers laminates overlapping leaves—
black, a smolder of yellow-green.

He curved his hands like wings, fingers tilting
convex to his palms, gliding through sleep.

New leaves, slightly red and sticky,
unfurl at the bottom of each twig,
a hand-held bouquet.

Translucent, they leap
a vernal moisture

and lick at the edge of vision,
though I look away.

The baby she lost
was asleep,
I go on hoping.

"When the world wasn't here,"
Matthew asks me, "what did the sky stay over?"
The grassy place we sit on rushes past.

The Persistence of Rain

for Matthew

They walk where fens exude cool mist,
each step pressing against the wind
that forces them back.

He tugs at her and will not look
at a lifeless squirrel on the trail.
She shoves it aside with her foot,
recoils from the clotted pelt.

Mom, he says, *don't ever die.*
Your body stays here but your soul
goes up in the sky. I want you to be
here, but not like that.

Under the pleasant crumble of leaf mold—
What's that stink? he asks.

It's skunk, she says, a lie. He persists—
Is that how dying smells?

She has no answer. They pass
squash with blossom-end rot,
tomatoes infected with tumors of smut.
The vines must be plucked and burned
or spores will multiply.

In a damp beard of ashes,
she builds a smoky bonfire
to dry their stubborn bones.

She shows him leaves, which blacken green
and never bleach to a fire-ready dryness—
each corn axil sprouts a tongue of cob.

What if the dead don't want to stay dead, he says.
Maybe they'll come back like corn—because of rain.

Tenancy

The River Refuses to Waive Its Lien

1.

January thaw: water trickles
from a nail hole in one kitchen beam.

February's rime reseals
shingles loosened by the snow rake.

March, the branches of five sugar maples
droop in the gutters of our roof.

Rooting in blown silt, box elder hulls,
these trees begin again, but higher.

2.

The old man, our neighbor—
no matter his hip pin, the weather—
poured tar on his flat roof.
He died of influenza.

I climb past the musky scents
of drains and muck to lilac, new
roof tiles on my shoulders.

I slip a little looking down
on the heads of my son and daughter;
a helicopter rescue crew is searching
the current for a boy we saw
drift by on a piece of ice.

3.

After you get your title free,
you find yourself on the island,
your lot at the small end of a spy glass.

You thought you'd settled on a hill.
In truth, your house survives
the steepest dropping off of an escarpment.

4.

The dam holds and a sandbar balds,
a rising isthmus beaver bridge
with saplings to the shore.

This is the spring an elk runs through your fence.
You sacrifice the aspen to your garden.

Ash Wednesday's here like a school girl
wearing a forehead smudge.

Canada geese swoop through
your unscreened soffit vents
to fly away with the roof.

Mississippi Requiem

1.

The stationary drought, our snare,
lured us from the shallows to the center,
where the muscular current twisted still,
and we heard the *Cheeee-ur– whit,*
whit, wheet of a cardinal.

2.

Boys threw a ball beyond the floats
dividing the swimming hole
from swifter swirl of rapids.
One so tall and frail, he was
his own shadow, black arms
reflecting the light.
In waist deep water,
squeamish feet on mire,
he hopped and skittered,
heedless of the river's pull.

3.

The clay receded
like unhealthy gums from teeth.
Boulders ringing the inlet
slid from the embankment.

4.

Even green-spotted turtles cracked their shields.
Solar grilling sucked their fluids, so they left
sunny logs to hide in sludge. Bottom dwelling
bull heads tore their bellies on the rocks.

5.

The great alluvial flood bed
formed a desert at each switchback.

Otters couldn't slide
baked wrinkles in the bank.

No spiral vallisneria, shining pond weed—
all dead in the steaming gumbo.
Desiccated reeds didn't rustle.

From the syrinx at the base of his wind pipe,
the red wing blackbird's song was weak,
his *kong-caree* less liquid.

6.

Sand choked the stranded clams.
The sturgeon's slack swim bladder failed him.
Scales softened on pumpkinseed and perch.
Maggots teemed beneath the carp,
exuding pong along the gravel.
The musk turtle's stench—
I turned her carapace over,
almost empty.

7.

Pursued by the sun,
I walked on the exposed
bed of shells and bones

then gasped and bent to touch
prints—a tiny human's!

No, the raccoon's
delicate fingers and toes.

8.

The boys threw their ball too far
and didn't wait for waves to slap it back,
as one by one they left the cove
to clamber over rocks to the sandbar,
forgetting currents cave
and hollow what they build.

9.

Then while tranced in a breast stroke,
I passed the drowning boy.
His cry, so faint, was gone
as I tried to turn and breach
the bright hard skin.
I couldn't dive
to drag him
from the bottom,
but why did I give up,
as if he died before he died?

10.

I couldn't mark the water
where it closed.
Annealing on his head,
the river shone like copper
between the earthen banks,
beneath the unrelenting sun.

January Candelabra

A woman uncovers compost,
discovers pit vipers wintering
in a braid under corn cobs.
She buries them in parings.

At midnight she finds a sloughed
honeycombed reticulated casing
from a last humped slithering,
cast like a firework worm's
cooled ash. Her fingers slide inside,
rose nails show through the scales.

When she wakes she feels the cold
as if her body were one long throat
in one slim sheath of flesh.
She leaves her cot as if it were her skin,
now wrong side out.

Snakes wait, no lids upon their stares.
They follow her, warm prey.
Like whips, in ever smaller loops,
they undulate her door sill.
Seething hisses wake her children,
who shiver but edge closer.

Sidewinding reptiles slink
single-file between bricks
and twine on the hearth over andirons,
touching from tongue to tail. They shake
scale beads—their serrate rattle mimics
the fire's lick and simmer.

The children gentle them,
stroke each venom gland
to glaze the brille upon their eyes,
before they ease the serpents down
to their mother. She never dared
to think she taught them this—
the way past fear.

How I Soared From a Ferris Wheel

for my children

It was your birthright to go
above the city, see how colors signal,
how people below are little
builders. Like sparrows
beaking confetti from trees for nests.
Even rats run high on wires
or dig in sewers.

I looked for your father,
so he would take you up
instead of me.
He didn't come,
so I had to be the one
with you. I was scared
of the creaking seats,
each rocking to a stop.

I imagined an air raft floating,
a lake breeze fanning us
as the great wheel rose—

"We're not afraid," you both told me.
"Open your eyes." So I did,
 just a slit,
the world between two feathers.

"You can't fall out," you insisted,
and I thought, *but you could fly.*

The Last Time I Defy This Yearly Death

Nine nights I've gone to harvest flax
in honor of the Equinox.

I garnered vases and cracked bowls
to scatter chartreuse zinnias,

cockscombs and blue-black gentians
on tables, ledge and bed.

Fireflies wink out,
but the waxing moon
flares on winter's long wick—
soon a waning candle.

Chrysanthemums and asters glimmer
plum and fuchsia by my fence—
I let their live coals murmur.

Trail Song for the Third Millennium

As a child grows, will she tally eagles,
starlings, grass—all lost to solar winds?

All she needs is on a raft.
Let the water carry her—

Water has endured,
though fathers dream of sulfur
and mothers cough all night,
springs soften hard pan clay,
where they must labor.

Mothers endure undoing
until eulogies. Tasks burgeon
like nettle under their feet.
Children blame them for stings,
absent fathers, subfusc lives.

Fathers endure withholding
until pockets are vacant;
the nothing they keep they spend
on fuel then deeper wells
to save their homes from fire.

Children endure diminishing
earth, air, minerals. They enjoy
noise—Tele-vision, tele-cell.
They twitter, never phone
or tell their parents they're afraid
to listen—The world's volcano hisses.

Dirt endures dilation and curettage,
gales, departing dust, the death of worms.
Miners scrape the humus from eluvium,
drills cutting deep to stone. Farmers sow
wheat in meager fields but harvest bones.

For now, the trees plant seeds, and leaves
spin the air we breathe, enduring

droughts, tsunamis, acid rain,
the poisoned cumulus,
broken membrane of the sky—
the searing azure.

Five Ways of Filling a Cup

for the parents of a child born with Cystic Fibrosis

1. *With Earth*

Water breaks from her womb for life,
as clouds exhale, loam breathes in,
and one child labors to overcome
the cavern's undertow,
the bloody inertia of birth.

2. *With Air*

Lakes and rivers inhale
the winds of oxygen
seined from rising hydrogen.
Vapor dries as it ascends.
Air circles the baby's lungs,
blossoming cups
of alveoli.

3. *With Water*

The water lily, its roots in marl, opens to air.
No bud, no girl with gills,
opens under water.

How can she live when air is trapped
and she is choking?

The nurse cups his hands on her back,
a percussion to loosen
the swamp in her lungs.

She expels the salty phlegm—
today it doesn't drown her.

4. *With Silence*

One soaring flute—a hermit thrush
shirrs the ozone, echoes
in your cup.

Set it, full of the empty
curve of stillness,
on your window sill.

If you do not cleave this cup,
you will not mend it.

Lay the shards
in the kiln of sun to meld;
then let it rain.

As you turn your cup,
may the river running in
pour out.

5. *With Fire*

California poppies are cups of flame.
Each blade of grass spits and crackles.
See the lightning, fields ablaze—
pitch smoke reaches the cupola,
peak of the pleural sac.

Cup your hands around
your nose and mouth,
your fiery breathing.

An Invitation to Diffusion

Go down to the water.
Imagine it narrows, a mirror
as you stand in current.
The river will open, if only you'll be
a flowering rush, a reed.

∞

Call your many selves from time
to meet in this coursing salmon run.
Perceiving the water, each other,
what will you become?

∞

Woman in the middle of your years,
dizzy when anything happens
the same way twice—
release yourself to eddies
melting into salmon scales,
broken and reformed,
a continuous sheet forever.

∞

Slantwise, you'll see farther—
yourself a girl: Naked feet sink deep
in quaking bog, sphagnum moss compressing.
Catapult from matted roots to a hummock island,
tethered to the shore with walking stones.

∞

As the sun on water angles lower,
and shadows lengthen on the strand,
be yourself the way an infant is—
know the flow with your skin.

∞

See the salmon entering a tidal bay
to swim upstream, old woman.

The bleeding Coho
lays her eggs in shallows.

You won't lose your fear of death
until, in a moment of forgetfulness,
you float downstream and leave
your body on the shore.

Fingerlings dart
to the sea.

Blake's Beautiful Failure

after Blake's visions and a print, Satan Inflicting Boils on Job

Men stacking sheaves complain of the heat. Above one tree
on Peckham Rye, the air is filled with a host of clear wings.

Below is William, a hunched engraver who pushes his burin[1]
to score *a line not drawn by chance*[2] in the copper plate:

Yahweh and snake entwine; devils are pulling Job below.
Soon they'll grab this ink-stained fool, old William.

Not the boy he was at nine years old—Will Blake,
who saw such visions! Gray-haired William weeps.

Like Job, he can't dispel devils or call prismatic angels.
He remembers a silver tree, bent low in a deasil[3] wind.

Angels multiply in rainbows for young Will. The Seraphim's toes
skim the hedgerow and glide the whitebeam's low crown,

slowing the spinning leaves. Again, old William sees
a downy nimbus around each leaf; hair ripples in sunless light.

As the tree uplifts its cargo, Cherubim unsheathe
the carmine scales on each unopened bud.

They peel the laurel-green shells, as thin
as the skin of William's eye lids,

revealing creamy nipples; petals of each flower
unfurl. Stars on trembling petioles throng branches,

replacing angels' feet—Thrones and Dominions[4] leave
but hover while petals fall. Will cries for fragrance and feathers.

William knows how ripeness turns to rot, how spent russet leaves
flame on dregs of grapes, called rape—only good for vinegar,

bad dreams: Ammonia fumes rise to old William's nose,
and he wakes Job before the fiends can chain him.

Men stacking sheaves complain of the heat. Above one tree
on Peckham Rye, the air is filled with a host of clear wings.

Worship in the Garden of Innocent Joy

after Blake's print, Night of Enitharmon's Joy

While William leads Catherine down a path of blue stone,
decent Lambeth people bow their heads in chapel.
Trumpet vines begin to climb the limestone wall.

Will unlaces the stays around his wife's soft waist—
A corset so cruel it even crushes her breasts,
and she inhales a breath so deep, he grins at her relief.

A priestess unrobes on Primrose Hill, to sway in holy dance
for Damara, goddess of fertility. Catherine takes off her petticoat.
William removes her shift, his shoes, and she unbuttons
his breeches; he tosses his shirt to a holly branch.

Loving skin to skin, they praise the gracile house of soul.
While they caress and gambol, the choir sings Hallelujah.
From the open chapel window, the rector thunders, "Eve's sin
is yours—the lure of the serpent's lascivious tongue!"

Trumpet flowers close and Catherine sleeps. William portrays her
awake in the night, her shoulders sheltering two lovers.
Above them, a golden-crowned flying fox—Chiroptera,
the queen of bats—purrs her wings. Below, an adder smiles.

Using Yahweh's bass voice, the rector grills Adam:
"how did you learn nakedness—who taught you shame?"
William yells, "The church!" and laughs as he limns the curve
of Catherine's thigh and tints her breasts rose madder.

William Blake Unmasks

after Blake's vision and a print, Satan Inflicting Boils on Job

When William's brother Robert rose
in his luminous body,
he clapped his hands for joy—
In such hurry for eternity,
he left his burin and brushes
and didn't say goodbye.

On Robert's bed, the bloody rags,
consumption handkerchiefs
that Catherine had to boil,
remain unwashed beyond his death.
William is summoning Rob's spirit.

She lays the table with her dowry, an empty dish
of Wedgwood blue in front of Will—he curses
but gets to work drawing the bare tureen.
Finished, he hides his face behind his plate—
a mask for commercial drudgery. He hacks
his sketches to a catalog to purchase flour and yeast.

Ignoring the light of Rob's emanation, Will sinks
in bleak vision—Job's sores suppurate, his face disappearing
beneath thick crusts. Blake has mercy and stoppers Satan's jug
of plague. He engraves a lion's muzzle on this fallen man.

His graver[5] cutting deeper in the plate, William suffers
the weight of Satan's feet on Job's groin and knee; the red
heft of Satan's pinions pushes down the bleeding sun.

William's candle gutters out, and he sees in gloom—the bright
sheets on his brother's bed, turned back for him. He sleeps
and wakes in a lucid dream: Rob etches into beeswax—
William's poetry. Seven Seraphim of the Presence[6]
sing, as masks melt from human faces.

In The Tunnel of Each Other's Eyes

for Stan

tall tasseled grass is flattened
by our footsteps, trailing shadows.

You falter by deep water,
facing a horizon I can't read,

codes that crows inscribe on sky
with sharp, whirring wings.

Fearing you release your life, our days,
to bleak skies, I weave your gaze with mine

until we see the Gulf's consuming blue, us two
curved against the slipface slide of dune,

embracing. Roots of salt-marsh hay
grip the shift and drift of sand.

A dragon fly's slowing, iridescent flight—
in pause, its multi-facet eyes perceive

a world in each grain of sand [7]
upon our naked bodies.

Years and miles farther, we kneel
before a tidal pool of sea stars.

Retrieval

The miscarried were no more
than a clam's itch on a sand grain:
layered, almost-pearls—
some to blastula, some to bone.
The mother who wanted them all had one:
"He slid right out and kept on going."

After childbirth, she finds in her comb
great gouts of hair. She should have buried
the placenta, which came as if by magic,
the living child a gift of that rich sponge.
His stay in the womb was usual, brief,
so pregnancy becomes her rumination.

Bezoars in the stomachs of llamas
take years. Metal filings turn true north.
A wood sliver works its way to upper skin.
A deer tick can be cut out. A blood clot
grows a membrane and is more
easily kept from the brain.

A stomach is a body's clearing house.
Can you blame it for keeping the trivial
flotsam, wheat or pine needles,
an artistry of indigestion,
arranged by lower powers
of camel and gazelle.

Accretions, stalactite growth. In this way
the body orders our real choices.
Encased in concentric resinous amber,
the bee glows still. Nothing is ever lost.

In the Long Dilation of Time and Space

1951

∞ *Winter Follows Summer in Milwaukee, Wisconsin*

My back to snow, the rusted chains
of a buried swing, I paint Mother Mary's robe.
Blue is brighter when I close my eyes. I know
you can't stop being created.

I pencil souls round as communion wafers
inside my family. Mom's pink face has tears.
Below are the bowls she broke at breakfast.

Dad hides his face with stubs of beard,
a razor cut—his hand is shaky
shaving for the mass called requiem.

I color me and my remaining brothers
with Crayola crayons, then float
a circle like the moon above us—

really Eddie, my little brother.
He dies when I'm not watching him
but doesn't go away.

1978

∞ *Night in Zurich, Switzerland*

My youngest brother, Tom, is late
by seven long days. Last heard from, he
was hiking God knows where in Lebanon—
still avoiding war? Or not.

That's the knot I cannot
loosen, the silent phone cord
I fray and twist, trying to untie my love
from burden. I'm not his mother
but sister, keeping the night watch.
I can only turn in bed, tangling my sheets.

∞ *Morning the Following Day*

I wake without weight, unafraid
and leave the phone behind to play
with my son in Belvoir Park.
He climbs a rose vine, thick
as his father's wrist, and pricks his finger.

When he touches a moth's wing,
it shimmers with dew and yellow pollen,
and he forgets to cry.

∞ *Evening*

Like a happy ending, Tom shows up for dinner.
As my husband toasts him, the phone brings Mom
crying in Milwaukee. Not for my brother's safe return,
but Dad's open heart—during surgery,
he almost dies but doesn't.
She says goodbye, not breaking
our connection.

My husband reminds me of my dream—
"You woke and asked if I called your name."
Then I recall a dark-caverned room, a man
silhouetted against a lamp, who bends
over a person draped in white,
lying on a table or an altar.

In deeper layers of lucidity,
someone tells me, "pray!" I am
useless, the one who isn't there in time.
I do not believe that prayer can save,
but still I pray through pain, a focus
on *lost* pushing through to *found*.

Always Now

The continuous moment occupies
no year, no place.

Still the family cabin sits
upon a quarry lake.

Voices reverberate
from cliffs of basalt, shale.

Each cadence and timbre
returns the same but changed—

our chorus interlaces
dissonance with grace notes.

Believe

This long grief   a dandelion's deep roots,
of your illness,   spiky leaves overtaking our lawn,

recovery,   a pale yellow maize,
which is death,   crowns fading to will-o'-the wisps,

will not hold   seeds floating on tensile filaments,
your spirit.

Survival

After the April blizzard,
we meet on the beach.
You torch the drift wood—
salt explodes in rainbows,
snow melt, steam and sizzle.
Lobsters hurtle down the dunes,
our kettle on the boil enough for all.

A man in pajamas brings a door
to sit on, our table. A girl finds wine
in rubble, and a boy holds a sea gull,
splinting its wing with his hands.
I'd live again for such a fire.

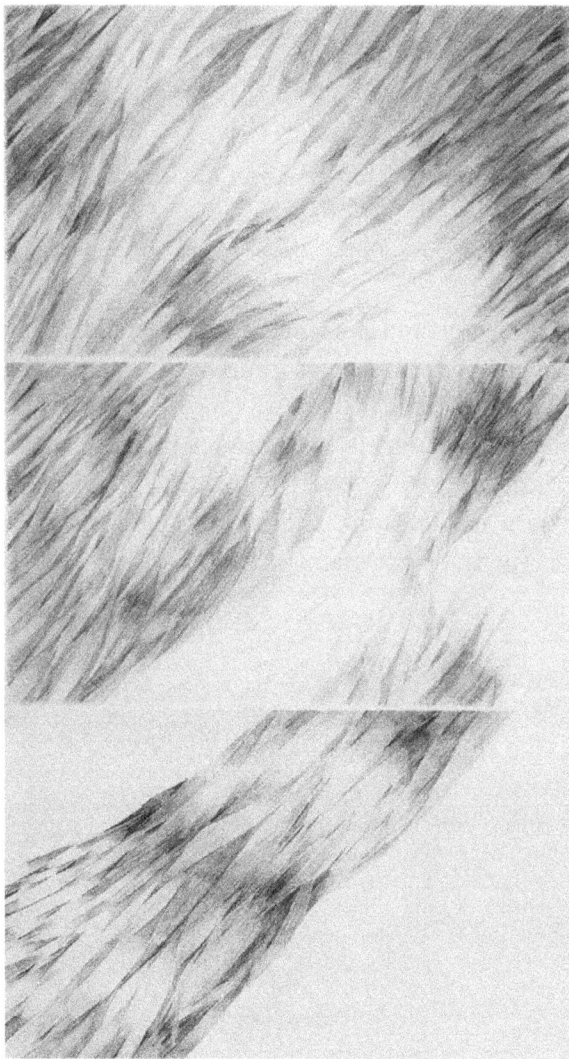

End Notes

1 A burin is an engraver's chisel.
2 A "line not formed by chance" is an elision of Blake's phrase in a letter.
3 Deasil refers to the wind's auspicious clockwise, or sun-path, direction.
4 Cherubim, thrones, and dominions are orders of angels.
5 A graver is an instrument for gouging lines or areas in a metal plate or block of wood.
6 In the nine orders of angels, seraphim, fiery ones, are the first angels of the highest order.
7 This line is a quote from William Blake's poem. "Auguries of Innocence" (penultimate stanza).

ABOUT THE AUTHOR

Patricia Barone has spent most of her life on the Mississippi River in Minnesota, where she lives with her husband, Stan. Although she was born in Gainesville, Texas, she grew up in Milwaukee, Wisconsin and lived for six years in New Orleans, Louisiana, and one year in Zurich, Switzerland.

Over the past three and a half decades, she has published widely in anthologies and periodicals: Most recently, a poem was published in *Inspired by Tagore*, a SAMPAD (South Asian arts) anthology published by the British Council of India. Her work has also appeared in Irish journals: *Revival* (Limerick Ireland), *The Shop* (County Cork, Ireland), and in *An Sionnach*, published under the auspices of the Irish Studies Department of Creighton University in Omaha, Nebraska. She has also published poetry in the Canadian journal, *Germination*. Her United States publications also include those in *And Magazine, Blue Buildings, Commonweal, Handbook III, Milkweed Chronicle, The Prose Poem Project, Ptolemy, Sidewalks, Sing Heavenly Muse!, Turtle Quarterly, Umbrella–Tilt a Whirl, West End, Widener Review*, and *Women's Quarterly Review*.

She received a Loft-McKnight Award of Distinction in poetry, chosen by Marilyn Hacker; a Lake Superior Contemporary Writers Award for the short story; and a Minnesota State Arts Board Career Opportunity Grant for a workshop with the Irish poet Eavan Boland.

Other Work by Patricia Barone

Books

Handmade Paper (a Minnesota Voices Award winner), New Rivers Press, 1994, a book of poetry nominated for a Minnesota Book Award

The Wind, a novella (a Minnesota Voices Award winner), New Rivers Press, 1987

Poetry in Anthologies

Inspired by Tagore (British Council of India, 2012)
Improbable Worlds (Mutabilis Press, 2011)
Shifting Balance Sheets, (Wising-Up Press, 2011)
The Wind Blows, The Ice Breaks (Nodin Press, 2010)
Sing Along the Way: Minnesota Women Poets From PreTerritorial Days to the Present (New Rivers Press, 2007)
The Talking of Hands, (New Rivers Press, 1998)
Going to the Lake, (Loonfeather Press,1996)
One Parish Over: Irish-American Writing, (New Rivers Press, 1993)
River Poems, Slapering Hol Press (The Hudson Valley Writer's Center, 1992)
Learning Language, (Prentice Hall, 1989)

Fiction in Anthologies and Periodicals

Daring to Repair, Wising Up Press, 2012
View From The Bed: View From The Bedside, Wising Up Press, 2010.
Becoming a Teacher in the New Society, Peter Lang, 2003
American Voices: Webs of Diversity, Prentice/Merrill, 1997
Bless Me Father, Plume/Penguin, 1995
American Writing, Nierika Editions, no. 5, 1992
West Wind Review, spring 1989

Printed in the United States of America

www.ingramcontent.com/pod-product-compliance
Lightning Source LLC
Chambersburg PA
CBHW022037090426
42741CB00007B/1095